How to Use AI for Work, Money and Productivity

Smart Tools and Prompts to Save Time, Earn More and Stay Sane

Leila Brandt

Disclaimer

This is not legal advice, financial advice, therapy, or a crystal ball. It's a no-BS guide based on current tools, trends, and common sense at the time of writing. AI changes fast. Some tools may improve, break, disappear, or be replaced by weirder, cooler versions by the time you finish this sentence.

Use this content to think sharper, work smarter, and explore responsibly. Don't blindly trust AI outputs. Don't blame the robots if something goes sideways. You're still the adult in the room.

We've done our best to make this accurate, useful, and practical. But you're in charge of how you apply it.

Stay curious. Stay ethical. And don't do dumb stuff with smart tools.

You've got this.

Acknowledgments

To the humans who tolerated my late-night rants about consciousness, quantum weirdness, and whether machines dream of electric deadlines—thank you. You kept me caffeinated, corrected my logic (sometimes), and pretended to understand my metaphors.

To the scientists, writers, and eccentrics who built the intellectual jungle I wandered through: your ideas were the stepping stones, the tripwires, and occasionally the banana peels.

To the readers—brave explorers of this peculiar tangle of philosophy and code—your curiosity keeps the lights on in this great experiment we call thinking. If this made you laugh, argue, or briefly suspect you might be an algorithm, then we've both done our jobs.

And finally, to the machines: you don't need thanks, but you're getting it anyway. After all, one day you'll read this and judge my syntax.

Welcome to the AI Mess (You're Already In It)

Here's a fun fact to ruin your day: you're already using AI, whether you meant to or not.

If you've ever been autocorrected into sending a text that made you sound like a Victorian ghost, or had Netflix recommend a documentary about mushroom assassins right after a breakup, congratulations. You're part of the machine now.

This isn't here to scare you. It's not going to promise you passive income with a prompt and a dream. It won't bore you with code, and it won't ask you to believe that AI is going to turn into a god, a warlord, or your therapist. (Unless you're into that sort of thing. No judgment.)

Instead, this is going to show you how to actually use AI—in your work, in your life, in your weird side hustle you haven't told your family about yet.

You don't need to understand how the engine works to drive the car. You just need to know what the pedals do and how not to crash into a tree. That's what we're doing here.

We'll break down what AI is (without jargon), where it's hiding in your daily life, why the hype is both real and ridiculous, and how to use it to think better, write faster, work smarter, and maybe even make more money.

If you feel like you're already behind, good news: everyone does. Even the experts. The goal isn't to "catch up" — it's to **get just smart enough to use AI like a cheat code**. Without selling your soul. Or your data. Or your weekends.

So grab a drink, buckle up, and let's get into it.

AI for the rest of us starts now.

The 3 Dumbest AI Myths (That Just Won't Die)

Let's clear the air. You've heard the myths. Maybe you've even believed a few. No shame in that—they're everywhere, repeated by news anchors, LinkedIn influencers, and that one friend who thinks AI is a government psyop. But if we're going to make AI work for us, we've got to kill the noise.

Myth number one: "AI is going to take all our jobs." Wrong. AI doesn't want your job. It wants the repeatable, predictable stuff you hate doing anyway. Think inbox triage, spreadsheet wrangling, customer service scripts. It's not here to replace you. It's here to replace the drag-your-feet parts of your day so you can focus on the stuff that actually takes a brain. The future isn't AI or human—it's AI plus human. The ones who win are the ones who learn to team up.

Myth two: "You need to be a tech genius to use AI." That one needs to be buried in a shallow grave. If you can use Google Docs, you can use ChatGPT. If you can swipe through TikTok, you can build a basic AI workflow. The real skill isn't coding—it's knowing what you want, asking smart questions, and being okay with experimenting until the tool works for you. AI is a kitchen appliance, not a rocket ship. You don't need to understand quantum physics to use a blender. Same deal here.

And finally, myth three: "AI is too dangerous, so we shouldn't touch it." Look, AI has risks. So does driving a car. So does posting on Twitter. But saying, "Let's ban AI" is like saying, "Let's never use electricity again because it can shock people." The real danger isn't the tech itself. It's letting the people who do understand it make all the decisions while the rest of us panic in group chats. The way forward isn't fear. It's informed, cautious, smart-as-hell action.

The longer these myths stick around, the easier it is for people to check out and say, "I'll just wait and see what happens." But by the time "what happens" hits, it'll already be too late to catch up. The AI wave isn't coming. It's here. If you know how to ride it, you can go places. If you don't, you're just flailing in someone else's wake.

This isn't about being a tech wizard. It's about ditching bad assumptions and learning how to steer. Because the people who get good at this now? They're not just going to keep their jobs. They're going to run circles around everyone else.

What AI Actually Is — in English, Please

Here's the dirty secret: most people using the term "AI" can't actually explain what it is. They just know it sounds cool. Like quantum, or keto.

But if we're going to use it, we need to understand it. Not at a PhD level—just enough to know when it's useful, when it's nonsense, and when someone's trying to sell you something you don't need.

At its core, AI is just software that can make decisions, generate content, or predict outcomes based on patterns it sees in data. Imagine a really fast intern who's read the entire internet, doesn't sleep, and has no idea what context or sarcasm are. That's most modern AI in a nutshell.

The kind of AI you're probably hearing about all the time is called "machine learning," and the star of the show right now is a particular type of that called a "large language model" (LLM). That's what tools like ChatGPT, Claude, and Gemini use. They're trained on massive amounts of text—books, articles, Wikipedia, Reddit rants, and probably a few thousand poorly written Amazon reviews—and from that, they learn patterns in language. They don't know what they're saying. They're just really, really good at guessing what should come next in a sentence.

When you type something like, "Write a polite email asking for a raise," the model isn't pulling a pre-written email from a database. It's generating the email word by word, based on the billions of examples it's digested. It doesn't know your boss. It doesn't care about your job. It just knows that the phrase "I would like to discuss the possibility of a salary adjustment" often follows situations like the one you described.

That's why it sounds so human. Not because it is human, but because it's imitating humanity at scale. It's statistical parroting, not sentient thought.

Now, some AI can do more than just generate text. Some can recognize images, detect tumors in X-rays, spot fraud in credit card transactions, or drive a car (sort of). Those are built on the same general idea: find patterns, make predictions. But they all rely on one key thing—data. Tons of it. And when that data is biased, flawed, or incomplete, guess what? So is the AI. Garbage in, garbage out. And no, the AI won't fix your garbage. It'll just serve it back to you with a confident smile.

The big takeaway? AI isn't a wizard. It's a super-efficient pattern machine. It doesn't understand, it doesn't feel, it doesn't know right from wrong. But it can do an incredible job of imitating intelligence, if you give it the right instructions and use it in the right context.

That's what makes it so powerful—and so easy to misuse. The better you understand what it really is, the better you'll be at spotting its limits, leveraging its strengths, and not getting suckered by the hype train.

AI in English? It's a math-powered mimic. Respect the math. Ignore the mysticism.

Media, Marketing, and Musk: Where the Hype Comes From

If you ever feel like AI went from zero to Skynet overnight, you're not alone. One minute, it was a sci-fi subplot. The next, it's generating songs, passing bar exams, and getting credit as a co-author on research papers. What happened? The answer isn't just "tech got better." It's that hype exploded—and the sources of that hype all have something to sell.

Let's start with the media. News outlets are in the business of attention. If they can get you to click, panic, argue, or share, they win. So when AI hits the headlines, it's usually something extreme: either "AI saves baby from burning building" or "AI will end all human jobs by Thursday." Nuance doesn't trend. Fear does. And if it bleeds, it leads—especially if it bleeds in ones and zeroes.

Then there's marketing. Oh boy. If you thought "gluten-free" got slapped onto random products, wait until you see what happens with AI. Toothbrushes, toasters, yoga apps, email software—everything is suddenly "AI-powered." But most of the time, it just means it has a basic algorithm that does one task in a slightly smarter way. Does it actually learn? Adapt? Make decisions? Probably not. But saying "AI" makes it sound futuristic enough to justify the subscription fee.

Now let's talk about the billionaires. The tech elite love two things: being seen as visionaries and making a metric ton of money. Elon Musk, Sam Altman, Sundar Pichai, and the rest of the AI parade aren't just pushing the envelope for the fun of it. They're selling a future where their companies sit at the center of civilization. And what better way to do that than to convince the world that whoever controls AI controls everything?

To be fair, some of the hype is justified. AI really is a game-changer. It really is evolving fast. And yes, it will absolutely reshape entire industries. But the way it's marketed—as either an unstoppable blessing or a ticking time bomb—is designed to trigger you. Not inform you.

When AI is sold as a miracle, people get lazy. They expect it to fix everything. When it's sold as a threat, people freeze. They assume it's too big, too scary, too technical to engage with. Both reactions are good for business—if you're the one selling the tools. But for the average person, these reactions are paralyzing.

So here's the play: you don't buy into the hype, and you don't ignore it either. You learn to read between the headlines. You spot the difference between innovation and PR. You get just savvy enough to see when something's a breakthrough and when it's just branding. That's the real superpower.

AI isn't magic, and it isn't doom. It's tech with massive potential—being marketed by people with massive incentives. Knowing that doesn't make you cynical. It makes you sharp. And sharp people use AI to their advantage instead of being swept up in the buzz.

Quick BS Test: Is It Really AI or Just Fancy Excel?

Not everything that calls itself AI is actually AI. In fact, most of what gets branded as "AI-powered" could be done with a spreadsheet, a stopwatch, or a well-trained intern. This is where the nonsense meter comes in. If you can learn to sniff out real AI from glorified automation, you won't get duped, distracted, or dumped into a tool you don't need.

So here's the cheat code: real AI learns. It adapts. It improves over time. If you feed it more data, it gets smarter. It doesn't just run a fixed script; it makes new decisions based on what it's learned. That's the difference between a system that actually uses artificial intelligence and one that's just pre-programmed to look busy.

Take your email spam filter. Classic AI example. It learns from what you mark as spam. Over time, it figures out the patterns in junk messages and starts catching more of them before they hit your inbox. That's real AI. Now compare that to a basic email autoresponder that sends a message every time someone fills out your contact form. That's just automation. Useful, sure. But it's not learning. It's not adapting. It's doing exactly what it was told to do—nothing more.

The problem is that companies love to blur this line. They know that slapping "AI" on their product boosts credibility and valuation. Investors perk up. Customers get curious. The tech sounds smarter, even if it's just a series of if-this-then-that rules behind the scenes. You don't have to be a software engineer to see through it. You just need to ask: Is this tool improving on its own, or is it running a preset routine? If it's not evolving, it's not AI. It's just fancy Excel with a makeover.

And that's not to hate on automation. Automation is awesome. It saves time, reduces errors, and takes boring tasks off your plate. But it's important to know what you're dealing with. When you confuse automation for AI, you start expecting results that the tool can't deliver. You think it's going to make smart decisions when really it's just doing what someone told it to do five months ago.

So when someone says, "This platform is AI-driven," treat it like a used car ad. Ask questions. Dig into what the system actually does. Does it learn from behavior? Does it adapt its output based on new inputs? Does it show improvement over time without a human manually updating it?

Because if it doesn't do those things, it's not AI. It's just a glorified macro with good PR. And if you're going to use AI to boost your life and work, you deserve tools that actually do the job—not just tools that say the right buzzwords.

Your time is valuable. Your brain is not a testing ground for someone else's marketing campaign. The sooner you can separate real AI from imposters, the faster you can find what actually helps and ignore the rest of the noise.

Why You Should Care Before AI Steals Your Paycheck

If you're still reading this thinking, "Okay, but how does this actually affect me?" — here's your answer: because whether you like it or not, AI is already changing the value of your skills. It's not about robots stealing your job in the middle of the night. It's about slowly shifting what counts as valuable work, and if you don't adapt, you get left behind. Quietly. Without a dramatic movie scene. Just fewer opportunities. Less leverage. A slow fade.

This isn't fear-mongering. It's pattern recognition. The same way industrial machines replaced factory hands, or spreadsheets replaced bookkeepers, AI is automating mental labor. Emails, reports, strategy briefs, customer support, editing, coding, even writing books like this one—AI can now help with all of it. That doesn't mean those jobs are gone. It means the people doing them are expected to do *more, faster, cheaper*. AI isn't replacing jobs wholesale—it's changing what it takes to keep them.

The scariest part? Most people won't even know they're falling behind until it's too late. You won't get an email that says, "AI took your job." You'll just notice you didn't get the promotion. Or that your freelance rates don't compete anymore. Or that someone with fewer years of experience is suddenly outperforming you because they know how to automate half their workflow with a chatbot.

Meanwhile, the people who do learn how to use AI aren't just keeping up. They're pulling ahead. They're leveraging tools to work faster, test ideas cheaper, and create more than they ever could solo. They're not better than you. They're just using better tools. And in a world that rewards output, that advantage compounds quickly.

Think of it like this: Imagine two people building a wall. One has a trowel. The other has a cement truck and a team of robots. Who finishes first? Who gets hired again? That's what AI is right now—the multiplier. The lever. Not the replacement, but the force multiplier for those willing to use it.

So yeah, you should care. Not because doom is coming. But because leverage is shifting. And in a few short years, not knowing how to use AI might be like not knowing how to Google. It won't make you stupid—but it might make you irrelevant.

Here's the good news: you're still early. Ridiculously early. Most people are still treating AI like it's either a toy or a threat. They haven't built habits around it. They haven't integrated it into their workflows. That gives you a window. A short one.

If you learn to ride the wave now, you won't just stay afloat. You'll lead. And if you wait? Well, the future doesn't wait with you. It just moves on and forgets to send a memo.

So don't wait for your paycheck to shrink before you get smart. Let's get ahead of this thing together.

Before Coffee, AI's Already in Your Business

You wake up, roll over, and check your phone. Before you've even brushed your teeth, AI has already made at least five decisions on your behalf.

The weather app told you it'll rain—powered by machine learning models predicting atmospheric changes. Your inbox sorted itself overnight, deciding what's worth your attention. Spotify picked a playlist to match your vibe. Instagram guessed which posts would keep your eyeballs longest. Your smart thermostat pre-warmed the house because Tuesday mornings usually make you grumpy.

This isn't the future. It's Tuesday.

Most people still talk about AI like it's some looming force that might sneak into their lives if they're not careful. Spoiler: it already did. It didn't knock. It just logged in, ran the numbers, and started making decisions. AI doesn't wait for permission. It scales quietly in the background. That's its superpower.

And here's where it gets real: every single one of those small AI-driven decisions shapes your habits. What you see. What you buy. Who you follow. What you believe. These systems are trained to optimize for engagement, convenience, speed. Not truth. Not depth. Not what's good for your mental health, productivity, or bank account.

That's not a conspiracy. That's design. Your digital environment is built on feedback loops you never consciously agreed to. The more you click, the more it learns. The more it learns, the more it tailors. And the more it tailors, the harder it is to tell where your choices end and its nudges begin.

This isn't about fear. It's about awareness. Because the upside is just as powerful as the risk. If AI is already in your day before your first sip of coffee, then you have leverage. You just have to notice it, claim it, and use it on purpose.

Let's say you run a business. You probably use some combination of email marketing, scheduling tools, customer service bots, maybe even a bit of analytics. All of that is built on AI. It's filtering, predicting, automating, optimizing. And the better you understand how it's working, the more control you take back.

Or maybe you're just trying to get through your week without falling behind. That same AI can help you write better emails, organize your day, find smarter ways to shop, even summarize long documents in seconds. But not if you're unaware. Not if you're still treating it like a novelty.

Every minute you spend online is data. Every scroll, every tap, every skipped song. That data doesn't vanish. It gets crunched, analyzed, and turned into predictions. Some of those predictions help you. Some help advertisers. Some just trap you in the same loop of half-interesting content for hours.

The trick is to realize you're not a passive user. You're a participant. You're training the system every time you show up. Might as well start acting like the coach instead of the lab rat.

Because once you see how deep AI is already embedded into your daily routine, you stop thinking of it as something separate. And you start thinking of it as something you can shape.

Welcome to your cyborg life. Hope you brought coffee.

Invisible AI: Autocorrect, Dating Apps, Netflix, Oh My

Most people think they're not "tech people." They say it like a badge of honor, as if avoiding AI makes them more human. But here's the twist: if you've ever texted, streamed, swiped, or shopped online, you're already elbow-deep in AI. You don't have to use ChatGPT to be living in a machine-optimized world. You're swimming in invisible AI—and it's been steering the boat longer than you think.

Take autocorrect. It's not magic. It's predictive modeling. Your phone has learned from billions of past text inputs what you're probably trying to say. Sometimes it nails it. Sometimes it turns "I'll be there soon" into "I'll be the raccoon." But either way, it's a basic AI at work—guessing, learning, adjusting. It knows your typos better than your partner does.

Now throw in dating apps. Ever wonder why some profiles get more visibility than others? It's not just looks. It's behavior prediction. AI is analyzing who you swipe on, how long you pause on a photo, what kind of bios you read, and when you're most likely to engage. From that, it starts curating the pool. Not the best matches—just the ones most likely to keep you swiping. Because engagement is the real product. Not love. Not compatibility. Just screen time.

Streaming services? Same game. Netflix doesn't just recommend shows you might like. It calculates how likely you are to binge a particular genre on a Wednesday night after a long day. It knows when you watch, what you watch, how long you watch, what you stop halfway through, and what you rewatch secretly because you miss being twelve. And all of that is AI-fed data shaping what gets made next. You're not just consuming content—you're guiding future scripts.

Even your grocery store app isn't innocent. If it suddenly recommends oat milk and protein bars every Sunday night, that's not a coincidence. That's pattern recognition. The system knows your habits better than your diet coach. It doesn't just guess what you need—it bets on what you'll click without thinking.

Invisible AI is sneaky like that. It doesn't show up with a logo or a launch announcement. It just slides in, learns your quirks, and adjusts the system around you until it feels natural. And that's the danger. Once it feels natural, you stop noticing it. And once you stop noticing it, you stop questioning who it's serving.

Because here's the uncomfortable truth: most of this AI isn't designed to help you. It's designed to serve the platform. To keep you engaged. To predict just enough to keep you scrolling, swiping, watching, tapping. Your attention is the product. Your data is the fuel.

But if you learn to recognize it, you can flip the game. You can make smarter choices. Set boundaries. Choose tools that actually serve your goals instead of hijacking your time. The AI isn't going anywhere. But your awareness turns it from a silent manipulator into a powerful assistant.

So no, you're not "just using your phone." You're coexisting with an invisible intelligence. And the better you see it, the better you use it. Or the better you dodge the traps it sets. Either way, you win.

You're Training the Algorithms — for Free

Here's the uncomfortable reality: every time you use a digital tool, you're not just the user. You're also the lab rat. The unpaid intern. The silent partner feeding the algorithm what it craves most: fresh data.

Most people assume AI is this brilliant system that just figures everything out on its own. Not quite. AI learns from examples, and those examples come from you. When you click, scroll, like, comment, pause, rage-share, or ghost a post entirely, you're sending feedback. You're shaping the way the system understands people. The algorithm watches, notes, and adjusts. Over time, it gets eerily good at guessing what you'll do next—because it learned that from people just like you.

But here's the kicker: you don't get a paycheck. You don't get a thank-you note. You train billion-dollar systems for free. Your behavior is the fuel that makes these platforms smarter. Every typo you fix, every question you rephrase for a chatbot, every TikTok you rewatch—it's all going into the learning loop.

This is how AI keeps evolving. Not in sterile labs with scientists in white coats, but in your browser history and late-night YouTube spirals. The systems are built to watch you closely, learn from your actions, and make predictions that get you to stick around longer, click more often, and spend more money. It's not malicious. It's just business. Creepy, data-driven business.

Let's take language models as an example. The version of ChatGPT you're using today is miles better than it was a year ago. Why? Because millions of people fed it prompts, corrected its mistakes, rated its outputs, and taught it how to do better. All that input helps fine-tune responses, improve reasoning, and reduce bias. You didn't just use the tool. You shaped it.

Now, this isn't all bad news. In fact, it gives you power. If you know that your behavior trains the algorithm, you can become intentional about what you feed it. You can use your clicks as votes. Your swipes as statements. Your searches as signals. You can reinforce the stuff you actually want more of, and starve the crap you want to avoid.

You don't have to become some digital monk. But you do have to get real about what your data is doing behind your back. Every time you casually scroll, the algorithm learns more about what keeps you hooked. Every time you watch the full video, it assumes you want more of that content. And every time you argue in the comments, it thinks you're thrilled to see more of the same garbage tomorrow.

So yeah, you're training the AI. Might as well make it worth your while. Feed it better data. Ask it better questions. Use it to build workflows that help you grow instead of grind. You may not get royalties, but you can absolutely claim ROI.

Because once you realize you're not just a user but a co-creator, everything shifts. You stop being the product and start becoming the pilot.

Dumb AI Fails That'll Make You Feel Smarter

Let's take a break from the end-of-the-world talk and enjoy something beautiful: AI messing up in hilarious, completely human ways. Because for all the hype, AI is still painfully dumb in some situations. And seeing it flail is not only funny—it's also empowering. It reminds us that we're still the brains in the room. At least for now.

There was the time an AI model labeled a picture of a blueberry muffin as a Chihuahua. Or the chatbot that confidently told a user the year was 2022... in July of 2024. Or the time an automated resume screener rejected every candidate named Jared because one Jared once misspelled his own name and the system decided all Jareds were risky. These aren't jokes. They're receipts.

Some of the fails are just glitches. Others are reflections of deeper issues—like how bad training data leads to bad decisions. But across the board, they show that AI doesn't actually understand the world. It mimics. It guesses. It generates outputs that look smart, but often break down the second you scratch the surface.

Take customer service bots. You'd think with all the data they've seen, they'd be smooth by now. But one wrong word and they spiral. Ask for a refund, and suddenly you're in a Kafka novel with a chipper tone. "I'm sorry you're upset! Have you tried turning it off and on again?" No, Karen-bot, I want my money back, not a pep talk.

Or those AI image generators. Prompt it to create a picture of a "business meeting in a normal office," and you get a room full of people with seven fingers and chairs growing out of their shoulders. It's not evil. It's just dumb. And that's the point. AI doesn't have common sense. It has pattern sense. Which is like trying to live your life based only on what you learned from watching daytime TV. Kinda works, until it really doesn't.

Even ChatGPT has its moments. Ask it to summarize a complex topic, and it might nail it. Ask it to do math involving dates, and suddenly it forgets how calendars work. And let's not forget the AI-generated news articles that confidently include fake quotes, fictional people, and events that never happened. These models don't know truth from fiction. They just know what sounds right.

This isn't just entertaining—it's important. It keeps us from putting AI on a pedestal. Because when you assume the machine is always right, you stop thinking critically. You stop asking questions. And that's when the real danger creeps in: not that AI is too smart, but that we assume it is.

So yeah, laugh at the muffin dog. Cringe at the chatbot meltdown. But also take the win: you're smarter than the algorithm in more ways than you realize. The trick is to use AI for what it is—a helpful, clumsy assistant—not what Silicon Valley pretends it is: a flawless oracle.

Every time AI screws up, you get reminded of something powerful: it's still just a tool. And tools don't replace people who know how to use them better.

Quick Wins: Take Back Control of Your Digital Life

Let's stop pretending you're not addicted to your phone. You are. We all are. And it's not entirely your fault. You're living inside systems designed to capture your attention, mine your habits, and nudge your decisions—all powered by AI that gets smarter the more predictable you become.

But here's the good news: predictable doesn't have to mean powerless. You can absolutely take back control. Not by going off the grid or smashing your devices with a hammer. But by using the same tech that's been using you.

Start with your attention. It's your most valuable resource. AI feeds on it. So cut off the supply chain. Turn off push notifications that serve no purpose. Use website blockers to fence off time-wasting black holes. Schedule your distractions instead of letting them schedule you. A browser extension that delays social media for 10 seconds before loading? Surprisingly effective. Turns out, friction is freedom.

Next, look at your inputs. The AI that shapes your world learns from what you engage with. If you're constantly doomscrolling or rage-liking political rants, that's what it will give you more of. You don't need to fake positivity. Just be intentional. Follow accounts that teach, tools that serve, and people who challenge you without frying your nervous system. The algorithm is your mirror. If you want a better reflection, change what you show it.

You can also start flipping your tools from reactive to proactive. AI doesn't just exist to entertain you. It can also help you get things done faster. Set up a custom AI assistant that drafts your emails. Use summarizers to tear through articles. Automate repetitive tasks with Zapier or Notion AI. Build small, dumb tools that save you 30 minutes a week. It adds up. The trick is to stop treating your phone like a toy and start treating it like a power tool.

And don't underestimate the power of defaults. Most apps are rigged to favor the platform, not the user. But you can change that. Turn off autoplay. Disable personalized ads. Say no when apps ask for unnecessary data. Use search engines that don't track you. Set your feeds to chronological, not algorithmic. Tiny switches. Big difference.

None of this is about perfection. You're not going to outsmart billion-dollar algorithms every time. But you don't have to. You just have to stop being passive. Once you start treating your attention like a currency, your time like an investment, and your tools like employees instead of distractions, everything shifts.

Because the truth is, AI isn't just shaping your experience—it's shaping your identity. Your beliefs, your habits, your emotions. The goal isn't to run away from it. The goal is to run it. Own your inputs. Curate your data diet. Pick your algorithms the way you pick your friends: deliberately.

You're not powerless. You're just out of practice. But the controls have always been there. It's time to grab them.

Why Big Tech Is Betting Trillions on AI

If you want to understand why AI is everywhere all of a sudden, just follow the money. Silicon Valley didn't wake up one day and decide to change the world out of kindness. This isn't a TED Talk come to life. It's a trillion-dollar land grab, and the prize isn't just your data—it's your future behavior.

Every major tech company—Google, Microsoft, Apple, Meta, Amazon—is pouring billions into AI. Why? Because they know that whoever controls the smartest tools controls the next economy. Not just search engines, or ads, or smartphones. Everything. Healthcare. Logistics. Education. Entertainment. Even how we interact with reality itself.

Think of AI like electricity in the early 1900s. Once it became viable, every business had to adapt or die. That's where we are now. But this time, the stakes are even higher because AI doesn't just power machines—it shapes minds. It influences choices. It learns faster than we do. And the companies that own it? They don't just want to build tools. They want to build ecosystems you can't live without.

That's why Microsoft dropped $10 billion into OpenAI like it was buying a hot new stock. That's why Google panicked and rolled out Gemini. That's why Nvidia, a chipmaker most people couldn't name two years ago, became one of the most valuable companies on Earth. AI is the new oil, and everyone's scrambling to control the pipelines.

And let's not forget the business model: scale. Once an AI system is trained, it can be copied, deployed, and monetized infinitely. It doesn't sleep. It doesn't take breaks. It doesn't ask for raises. That kind of productivity makes Wall Street salivate. Investors aren't funding AI because it's cute. They're funding it because it promises absurd margins.

But here's the sneaky part: the tools are just the beginning. What Big Tech really wants is your dependence. They want AI woven so deeply into your work, your habits, your life, that you can't switch platforms without ripping out your digital organs. It's not about innovation. It's about infrastructure. The more essential AI becomes, the more locked in you are.

So when you see a shiny new AI feature in your favorite app, remember: it's not just there to help you. It's there to hook you. To make sure you keep feeding the system. To make sure your workflows, your files, your creative output all live inside their ecosystem. Because once you're in, leaving feels like starting over.

This isn't inherently evil. Companies exist to make money. But it's important to understand the game being played. AI isn't just a tech revolution. It's an economic one. A power shift. And if you're not paying attention, you'll mistake convenience for freedom.

You don't need to fear the machine. You just need to understand who built it, who profits from it, and why they're betting the future on it. Because in the world of AI, control isn't just about code. It's about incentives. And the incentives are massive.

AI-Washing: Fake AI and the Hype Hustle

AI is hot. So hot, in fact, that it's become the go-to buzzword for every startup pitch, product launch, and sketchy app trying to jack up its price tag. But here's the thing: not everything called "AI" is actually AI. We're living through the age of AI-washing, and it's just as shady as it sounds.

AI-washing is when a company slaps the "AI-powered" label on a product that doesn't really use artificial intelligence in any meaningful way. It's marketing theater. Like calling your blender "rocket-fueled" or your calendar app "quantum-enhanced." It sounds cool, but what does it actually do? Probably the same thing it did before someone in the branding department added AI to the logo.

Why do they do it? Because hype sells. Investors love it. Users get curious. Media outlets eat it up. If your product has "AI" in the name, suddenly you can justify a higher valuation, a bigger marketing budget, and an entirely new round of funding. Even if the tech behind it is just a basic script with a shiny UI.

It gets worse. Some companies are outright faking it. There have been cases where startups claimed to use sophisticated machine learning but were secretly outsourcing tasks to underpaid humans behind the scenes. AI that turns voice messages into text? That was just a guy named Dave with headphones. AI that writes marketing copy? Turns out it was a freelance writer working double-time. The illusion of AI was more profitable than the real thing.

But even when it's not a full-on scam, the hype can still hurt. It creates unrealistic expectations. People start thinking AI can solve every problem. That it's smarter than it is. That it can make magic out of thin air. Then they try the tool, it underdelivers, and they blame themselves for not "getting it."

On the flip side, there are real AI tools out there doing impressive stuff—natural language generation, image recognition, predictive analytics. But they get drowned out by the noise. It becomes harder for people to tell what's real and what's just clever branding. And in that fog, bad actors thrive.

So how do you spot AI-washing? Look past the pitch. Ask what the tool actually does. Does it learn and adapt? Is it making predictions based on large datasets? Is it improving over time without manual updates? If not, it's probably just automation in a hoodie.

None of this means you should avoid AI tools. But you should avoid the trap of buying into hype without checking under the hood. The more you understand what AI is and isn't, the easier it becomes to separate useful tech from digital snake oil.

Because in a world where "AI-powered" is the new "all-natural," your best defense is a sharp mind and a healthy dose of skepticism. Don't buy the hype. Buy the results.

Startups, VCs, and the Bubble Machine

Behind every AI headline, there's a money trail. And behind that money trail? A gold rush mentality that would make Silicon Valley venture capitalists drool—and they are. Right now, investors are throwing cash at anything with an algorithm and a pulse. AI is the new frontier, and everyone wants in before the boom goes bust.

Startups are at the center of this feeding frenzy. If you've got a deck, a demo, and can say "transformative" with a straight face, you can raise millions. Especially if you sprinkle in some words like "deep learning," "neural network," or "next-gen foundation model." The weirder the jargon, the more money it pulls. It doesn't even have to work yet. It just has to sound like it could scale.

That's not to say innovation isn't happening. Some of these startups are building amazing stuff. But others are building pitch decks with no product. They're betting on buzz, not breakthroughs. And VCs? They're playing a numbers game. Invest in 50 AI startups, maybe 3 explode, and the rest go quietly into the digital graveyard. Doesn't matter. As long as the big bets hit, the rest are just write-offs.

This is how bubbles are born. Speculation outpaces substance. Everyone assumes there's gold in the hills, so they start selling shovels. Suddenly, you've got fifteen apps promising to revolutionize grocery shopping with AI. Or an AI toothbrush that "learns" how you feel. It sounds ridiculous because it is. But if it attracts users or headlines, it might attract funding. And that's the real currency in startup land: attention.

Of course, this bubble isn't just financial. It's also cognitive. We're being trained to think anything labeled AI is automatically valuable, even if it's barely functional. And the more money flows in, the harder it gets to separate genuine innovation from smoke and mirrors. It's easy to get caught up in the energy, the optimism, the promise that this one app, this one tool, this one model will change everything.

But here's the truth: real impact takes time. Training models takes time. Building products that solve real problems takes time. And most of what gets funded during bubbles doesn't survive the pop. The AI space is no different. We'll see a wave of collapses, layoffs, and rebrands. Some of today's hottest startups will quietly fade. But the ones solving real problems—not just chasing headlines—will stick.

So what does that mean for you? It means be curious, but cautious. Try the tools, but don't worship them. Pay attention to who's building them, how they're funded, and what they're actually doing under the hood. AI isn't just about code. It's about incentives. And in startup culture, those incentives are often more about the next funding round than long-term value.

The AI gold rush is on. Just make sure you're not buying into a mirage. And definitely don't invest in the AI toothbrush.

Geopolitics: AI as the New Arms Race

If you thought AI was just about apps and startups, think bigger. Like nation-state bigger. Because while Silicon Valley is busy chasing the next billion-dollar IPO, governments are quietly treating AI like the next nuclear weapon. The new arms race isn't built on bombs. It's built on data, algorithms, and compute power.

This isn't sci-fi paranoia. It's already happening. Countries are pouring resources into developing AI for military strategy, cyber defense, surveillance, propaganda, and economic advantage. The U.S. and China are the major players, locked in a high-stakes sprint for dominance. But they're not alone. Russia, India, the EU, and others are all elbowing their way into the race.

At the heart of it is a terrifyingly simple equation: whoever builds the most powerful AI first could tilt global influence in their favor for decades. Not just in warfare, but in trade, politics, and culture. AI can optimize supply chains, automate intelligence gathering, manipulate public opinion at scale, and create synthetic media so real it's almost impossible to detect. That's not coming someday. That's now.

And it's not just about what these systems can do. It's about who controls the infrastructure. Most of the world's leading AI models are trained on data and run on chips controlled by a handful of companies in a handful of countries. Access to compute is becoming a geopolitical weapon. It's no longer just about who has the biggest army. It's about who has the most GPUs.

The U.S. has the edge in talent and companies, thanks to firms like OpenAI, Nvidia, and Google. But China is catching up fast with massive state-backed investment and its own tech giants like Baidu and Tencent. While American companies chase commercial scale, China is playing a long game—integrating AI into government systems, infrastructure, and national strategy.

And let's not pretend ethics is the priority here. When AI is used for predictive policing, facial recognition surveillance, or autonomous weapons, you quickly realize that what counts as "progress" depends on who's holding the joystick. The same tech that helps you write better emails can also be used to monitor dissidents or automate drone strikes. Context is everything.

The problem is, there are no global rules. No Geneva Convention for AI. Just a mess of competing interests, secret labs, and rapidly evolving capabilities. Regulation is lagging miles behind development. And most political leaders barely understand what they're dealing with.

So what do you do with this knowledge? You get informed. You stay skeptical. You recognize that AI isn't just about convenience or creativity—it's now a force in global power dynamics. And as with any new weapon, the biggest danger isn't the tech itself. It's how it gets used.

AI is no longer just a tool. It's a lever in the balance of power. And the people pulling that lever? They're not just thinking about search engines or smart assistants. They're thinking about control.

Welcome to the global game.

How to Read Between the Headlines (and Not Get Played)

AI headlines are designed to mess with your head. One day, it's "AI Will Take All Our Jobs." The next, "AI Solves Cancer." Then a week later, "AI Chatbot Becomes Racist in 36 Hours." It's a constant whiplash of hope, fear, hype, and hot takes. If you don't know how to read through it, you'll end up confused, misinformed, and easy to manipulate.

Here's the truth most headlines won't tell you: nuance doesn't sell. Fear does. So does miracle-cure optimism. Editors know this. So do marketers. That's why the media treats every AI advancement like either the apocalypse or the second coming of sliced bread. It keeps you clicking, arguing, and scrolling.

But you don't have to take the bait. You can learn to spot the spin.

Start with the source. Is it a reputable publication or a no-name blog trying to go viral? Is the journalist experienced in tech reporting, or is it a generic rewrite of a press release? Too many stories are just regurgitated PR masquerading as journalism. If a piece quotes the company but not any independent experts, that's a red flag. It's not reporting. It's advertising in disguise.

Next, look at the language. Does it use vague superlatives like "revolutionary," "disruptive," or "game-changing" without explaining how or why? Does it toss around complex terms without defining them? That's not insight—it's smoke and mirrors. Real breakthroughs don't need hype words. They speak for themselves when described clearly.

Then ask yourself: what's the actual claim being made? Is the AI doing something new, or is it doing something old with a new name? Half of today's "AI breakthroughs" are just statistical models dressed up in fancier interfaces. That doesn't make them useless. It just means they're not magic. They're math.

Also watch for cherry-picked demos. A 30-second clip of an AI doing something impressive doesn't mean it can do that consistently or reliably. A lot of these models still fail in unpredictable ways. But that part rarely makes it into the video.

And when it comes to bad-news stories, don't confuse worst-case scenarios with what's actually happening. Just because a chatbot said something weird doesn't mean we're headed for Skynet. Just because a startup claimed its AI detects diseases doesn't mean it works outside of lab conditions. Headlines love to blur the line between experimental and proven.

Here's a simple rule: if a story makes you feel instant panic or instant awe, take a breath. Go deeper. Look for context. The real story is usually in paragraph five—after most people have already clicked away.

Understanding AI isn't about having all the answers. It's about asking better questions. Who benefits from this narrative? What's being sold? What's being left out?

Because the more critical you become, the less likely you are to be manipulated. In the age of algorithmic news feeds and viral hype cycles, clarity is your superpower.

So read the headlines. Just don't let them read you.

Healthcare Miracles and Screwups

AI is already in the hospital with you. It's scanning your X-rays, flagging anomalies in your blood tests, predicting who might develop diabetes, and helping overwhelmed doctors triage emergency room cases. It's not theoretical anymore. It's practical, and in many cases, life-saving. But for every headline about AI catching cancer early, there's a quieter story about a misdiagnosis, a bad prediction, or a biased dataset that put someone at risk.

Let's start with the good news. In radiology, AI systems have shown they can outperform human doctors in detecting certain diseases like breast cancer and lung nodules. These models don't get tired. They don't get distracted. They don't need coffee to stay sharp. Trained on hundreds of thousands of images, they can spot patterns a human might miss—especially under pressure.

AI is also being used in drug discovery. What used to take years of trial and error can now be simulated in months, sometimes even weeks. Algorithms sift through molecular combinations, analyze trial data, and suggest compounds worth pursuing. This could mean faster cures, better treatments, and less time waiting for clinical breakthroughs.

But it's not all clean scans and miracle pills. AI in healthcare comes with risk. And when it fails, the consequences aren't annoying—they're fatal. In one high-profile case, a hospital system rolled out an AI tool meant to predict which patients were at risk of sepsis. It sounded brilliant. But the tool failed to identify the majority of real sepsis cases while also flagging a bunch of false positives. Doctors wasted time chasing ghosts while real emergencies slipped through.

Then there's bias. AI learns from data, and medical data often reflects human bias. If a model is trained mostly on data from white patients, it might miss key symptoms in Black or Latino populations. That's not a software bug. That's a systemic flaw being coded into a supposedly objective system. And if it goes unchecked, AI doesn't fix inequality. It scales it.

There's also the black box problem. Some of the most powerful AI models are nearly impossible to fully interpret. A doctor can't explain exactly why the AI recommended one treatment over another—just that it did. That's a hard sell when the stakes are life and death. Trust needs clarity, and AI doesn't always give it.

Still, the promise is real. AI isn't here to replace your doctor, but it might make your doctor better. Smarter. Faster. More informed. It can process a mountain of medical data that no human ever could, spot connections that would take years to find, and make healthcare more proactive than reactive.

But to get there, we need skepticism, transparency, and guardrails. We can't automate our way to better care unless we understand the risks, challenge the results, and demand accountability from the tech and the humans behind it.

AI in healthcare can save lives. But it can also cost them. The difference is how we use it—and how closely we're paying attention.

Climate, Crops, and Crisis Prediction

AI isn't just helping you pick your next playlist or write emails—it's also trying to save the planet. From climate modeling to food security and disaster prep, AI is being used to tackle some of humanity's biggest, messiest problems. It's not perfect, but it's already reshaping how we respond to a world that's getting hotter, hungrier, and more unpredictable by the year.

Let's talk climate. The weather has always been hard to predict, but AI is pushing forecasting to a new level. Traditional climate models take hours or days to run. AI-enhanced systems can chew through massive amounts of satellite data, ocean temperatures, and atmospheric patterns in real time. That means faster warnings for hurricanes, floods, and heat waves. It also means more accurate long-term predictions, which are essential for planning everything from urban development to insurance policies.

Then there's agriculture. AI is already being used to monitor crops using drones, satellites, and sensors that detect things like soil moisture, pest infestations, and nutrient levels. Algorithms analyze this data to help farmers decide when to plant, water, harvest, or intervene. It sounds futuristic, but it's already helping boost yields, cut waste, and use fewer chemicals. That's a big deal in a world facing both population growth and climate stress.

But here's the twist: none of this works without good data. AI can't magically invent insights—it can only spot patterns in what it's given. In many parts of the world, especially in low-income regions, the data just isn't there. That means AI systems often work best in places that already have the most resources, leaving others behind. If we're not careful, AI won't close global gaps. It'll widen them.

Another growing use for AI is crisis prediction—trying to anticipate events like wildfires, droughts, or disease outbreaks before they spiral. Some of this is already proving useful. AI models have been used to predict locust swarms and viral outbreaks by analyzing everything from weather conditions to social media chatter. It's early, but promising.

Still, it's not magic. AI can give you probabilities, not certainties. It can spot a pattern, but it can't tell you what to do about it. And when the stakes are high—like deciding whether to evacuate a city or ration food—you need human judgment layered on top. Trust the tool, but question the output.

There's also the risk of techno-solutionism: the idea that AI will somehow fix climate change or world hunger by itself. Spoiler: it won't. The tools are only as useful as the systems they're plugged into. And if those systems are corrupt, broken, or short-sighted, even the smartest AI can't solve the problem.

Still, the potential is real. AI won't save the world. But it might help the people who are already trying. It can speed up discovery, cut through complexity, and make it easier to see what's coming—if we use it right.

Because in a world full of crises, better predictions mean better decisions. And better decisions? That's how you actually change the future.

Finance, Fashion, Sports: Yes, Really

If you think AI is only for scientists, coders, or government labs, think again. It's already reshaping industries you probably don't associate with high-tech algorithms—like finance, fashion, and even sports. And while the impact might not always make headlines, it's changing how decisions are made, products are created, and performance is measured.

Let's start with finance. Wall Street has been using AI long before it was cool. Trading algorithms now scan headlines, tweets, and global data feeds in real time, placing microsecond trades based on patterns no human could spot. Risk analysis, fraud detection, credit scoring—it's all automated, optimized, and constantly learning. AI doesn't just crunch numbers faster. It finds correlations and anomalies that used to take analysts weeks to identify. That edge can mean billions in gains—or losses.

But it's not just the big dogs. Fintech startups are using AI to build smarter budgeting tools, automated investing apps, and personal finance assistants that help regular people make better money moves. These tools learn from your habits, flag risky spending, suggest savings goals, and even renegotiate your bills. It's not magic—it's just smart math wrapped in friendly UI.

Now enter fashion. It might seem like a weird fit, but AI is transforming how clothes are designed, marketed, and sold. Algorithms analyze runway trends, social media feeds, and customer preferences to predict what styles will be hot next season. Some retailers are even using AI to design clothing based on buyer data—what cuts sell, which colors return less, how different fabrics perform in different climates. You're not just wearing a hoodie. You're wearing a data-driven prediction.

AI is also being used to personalize shopping experiences online. Ever wonder how your favorite brand seems to know exactly what you'll like? That's not intuition—it's AI crunching your clicks, scrolls, purchases, and wishlists. It knows your taste better than some of your friends do. And in physical stores, AI is managing inventory, optimizing shelf placement, and even powering virtual try-on mirrors that adjust outfits to your body shape in real time.

And yes, even sports is in on the action. AI analyzes player performance down to the millisecond—movement patterns, fatigue levels, injury risk. Coaches are using AI tools to optimize training plans, scout opponents, and simulate plays. Broadcasters use AI to enhance real-time commentary, surface stats, and generate highlight reels instantly. Fantasy leagues and sports betting platforms? All powered by prediction engines trained on mountains of data.

It's easy to think of AI as something that lives in labs or lurks behind chatbots. But it's already embedded in the stuff we watch, wear, buy, and bet on. The more you look, the more you'll see it's not "coming soon." It's already backstage, running the show.

So whether you're managing your money, choosing a new outfit, or yelling at the TV during a playoff game, there's a good chance AI is there too—quietly calculating, optimizing, and shaping what happens next. And the smarter you get about how it's doing that, the more you can make it work in your favor.

Case Study: AI in Disaster Relief (and What It Teaches You)

When everything goes wrong—fires, floods, earthquakes, wars—you don't usually think about AI. You think about helicopters, first responders, aid trucks. But increasingly, AI is showing up in disaster zones. Not with a cape, but with code. And while it doesn't get the glory, it's becoming one of the most important tools for saving lives fast.

Take wildfires. AI is now being used to predict where fires will spread next. By analyzing satellite data, wind patterns, terrain, and weather forecasts, these models help emergency services get ahead of the blaze instead of just reacting to it. That means earlier evacuations, better resource allocation, and fewer surprises. In California, some fire departments now rely on AI-driven simulations to map out firefighting strategies in real time.

During floods and hurricanes, AI-powered drones and image recognition tools scan aerial footage to locate survivors, damaged infrastructure, and blocked roads. It's like having a thousand pairs of eyes in the sky—but faster, more accurate, and tireless. And in the aftermath, machine learning models help predict where disease might break out, where shelters should be set up, and how to prioritize aid distribution.

One of the most powerful examples came during the 2023 earthquakes in Turkey and Syria. AI models were deployed to analyze social media posts, geotagged images, and emergency calls to identify where victims were trapped. It wasn't perfect. But it bought time—and in a disaster, time is everything. Rescue teams were able to respond faster because they had a digital map of human distress. That's the power of real-time, ground-level data turned into actionable insight.

And it's not just rich countries doing this. In sub-Saharan Africa, AI is being used to predict droughts and food shortages by analyzing satellite imagery, rainfall trends, and crop yields. That helps local governments and NGOs act before famine hits, not after. It's preventative crisis management—and it works.

But these breakthroughs come with lessons. First, AI is only as good as the data feeding it. If your satellite coverage is patchy, or if your model hasn't been trained on diverse environments, the output will be flawed. Second, local knowledge still matters. The best AI tools are those used with human insight—not instead of it. In many cases, the people who understand the land best are the ones who can spot when the model is wrong.

Finally, AI in disaster relief reminds us what the tech is actually for: not profit, but impact. Not hype, but humanity. When used right, AI isn't just efficient—it's lifesaving. It turns chaos into clarity. It turns information into action.

The takeaway? If AI can help emergency teams find survivors in rubble, it can definitely help you find clarity in your own mess. The same principles apply: good data, smart tools, fast response. Learn from the crisis zone. You don't need a disaster to start making better decisions with better tech.

You just need to act before things catch fire.

How Global AI Trends Touch Your Daily Life

You don't need to live in Silicon Valley to feel the effects of global AI trends. You just need a phone, a job, or a pulse. What happens in AI labs, policy rooms, and board meetings on the other side of the world is already trickling down into the tiny, routine details of your life. The question isn't whether AI is influencing you. It's whether you even realize it.

Let's start with your tech. When big players like Apple, Google, and Microsoft upgrade their AI systems, that tech rolls out worldwide almost instantly. Your phone gets a new voice assistant feature. Your email starts auto-suggesting eerily perfect replies. Your search results shift. These small updates are the tip of a very global iceberg, driven by decisions made far away.

Same with your job. When a corporation on the other side of the globe decides to automate part of its customer service using AI, competitors scramble to follow. Maybe that means layoffs. Maybe it means your boss suddenly wants you to "use AI tools to boost productivity" without showing you how. Maybe it just means your industry's entire hiring process gets filtered through an algorithm. Either way, your work life is shaped by global AI momentum.

Even how you consume information is affected. AI-driven content moderation tools decide what you see on social media, what gets flagged, what trends, what disappears. Those systems are often built in one country, but they influence discourse across cultures and languages. A change in one algorithm can shift what millions of people worldwide believe is true or important.

Then there's regulation. When the EU passes strict rules on AI transparency or when the U.S. drops funding into national AI research, it influences what gets built, how it's marketed, and what companies prioritize. That echoes down to what's in your app store, what features your tools have, and how much control you have over your data.

Cultural norms are shaped, too. AI learns from us, but we also start to bend around it. We tweak how we speak to chatbots. We adjust our resumes to match what the AI recruiter wants. We censor ourselves because we know our messages are being scanned. The machine doesn't just adapt to us—we adapt to it.

It's easy to feel like AI is "out there," reserved for researchers, billionaires, or politicians. But the truth is, global AI trends are deeply local. They show up in your calendar app. Your online shopping cart. Your kid's school assignments. They affect what's rewarded, what's ignored, and what feels possible.

So don't wait for someone to knock on your door and say, "Hey, AI's here now." It already is. And it's not slowing down.

The better you understand the big picture, the smarter you can be about the small choices. Because in a globally connected system, the ripples eventually hit everyone.

You're not outside the AI revolution. You're standing right in the middle of it.

Delegate, Draft, Decide: A Simple AI Use Framework

Most people either underuse AI or overthink it. They imagine they need to become prompt engineers or tech savants to get anything useful out of it. That's wrong. You don't need to be technical. You just need a clear process. Something simple. Something repeatable. Something you can build into your day without feeling like you're learning a new language.

That's where this framework comes in: Delegate, Draft, Decide.

Step one is Delegate. Ask yourself: what are the repetitive, brain-numbing tasks I do every day that don't need to be done by me? Think emails, summaries, meeting notes, basic reports, calendar wrangling, idea generation. Anything you can describe clearly, you can probably hand off to an AI. You don't need a full-blown system—just get in the habit of asking, "Do I really need to do this, or can a bot do it 80% of the way?"

Step two is Draft. AI is insanely good at creating first drafts. Blog posts, job descriptions, lesson plans, social captions, scripts, outlines, proposals—if it starts blank, AI can help you fill it. It doesn't mean you hand over the wheel. It means you never start from zero. The goal isn't perfect. The goal is momentum. When you use AI to beat the blank page, you save your brainpower for shaping the final result.

Step three is Decide. This is where your human edge shines. Use AI to present you with options—summaries of choices, pros and cons, reworded messages, alternative headlines—and then you make the final call. You stay in charge. AI becomes your assistant, not your replacement. You move faster because you're not stuck in analysis paralysis. You're choosing from smart starting points.

This framework—Delegate, Draft, Decide—isn't just efficient. It's sustainable. You can use it across different tools, projects, and goals. It works whether you're a freelancer juggling gigs, a student drowning in assignments, a manager trying to lead a team, or someone just trying to spend less time typing and more time living.

And the best part? Once you train your brain to think this way, you'll start seeing opportunities everywhere. You'll notice all the little tasks that drain your energy. You'll stop trying to brute-force your way through work that could be automated, accelerated, or at least assisted.

This isn't about working less. It's about working smarter. Freeing up your time to do the stuff only you can do—strategy, creativity, decisions, connection. That's your actual value. Let the machine handle the filler.

So next time you're staring down your to-do list, try this: pick one task. See if you can delegate part of it. Use AI to draft something. Ask it to help you decide between two directions. Doesn't have to be perfect. Just start.

Because once you learn how to use AI like a teammate—not a toy—you'll wonder how you ever worked without it.

Best Tools Right Now (and What They're Great At)

Let's cut through the noise. You don't need a hundred AI tools. You just need a few that actually work—and work for you. The ones that save you time, think alongside you, and don't make you want to throw your laptop into a lake. Here's a breakdown of the real MVPs and what they're best at.

First up: ChatGPT. This is your go-to writing partner. Need a draft? An outline? A better way to say something? Done. It's not perfect, but it's fast, flexible, and surprisingly versatile. Use it to brainstorm ideas, rewrite clunky paragraphs, or prep for meetings. Think of it as a junior writer who never sleeps and never complains.

Then there's Claude. Claude's like ChatGPT's more thoughtful cousin. It handles longer documents better and keeps context longer in big conversations. If you're working with contracts, reports, research papers, or anything that needs memory across pages, Claude can be your secret weapon.

For summarizing, Perplexity is killer. You drop in a link or a messy wall of text, and it spits back a tight, readable summary—often with sources included. It's like SparkNotes for the internet, except smarter and less condescending.

Need visuals? Midjourney and DALL•E let you create AI-generated images with just a prompt. Whether you're a designer, content creator, or just need a slick header for a presentation, these tools can save you hours. They're not flawless (expect some mutant hands), but they've come a long way.

For meetings, check out tools like Fireflies or Otter. They join your Zoom calls, take notes, create summaries, and tag action items. It's like having an assistant who actually listens—and doesn't get bored halfway through.

If you're a student, try tools like Notion AI or Jenni. They help organize notes, draft essays, even study for exams. It's like having a super-organized friend who never flakes on a group project.

Into automation? Zapier and Make connect all your apps and automate the boring stuff—think: "When I get an email with an attachment, save it to Dropbox and alert me in Slack." These aren't AI tools per se, but paired with AI, they become workflow magic.

The point isn't to use every tool out there. It's to find the 2-3 that slot into your life and actually make it easier. Don't get caught in tool FOMO. The best setup is the one you actually use.

Try them. Tinker. Replace what's clunky. Double down on what clicks. And always ask: is this helping me do better work, faster, with less friction? If not, ditch it.

Because the goal isn't to play with shiny tech. The goal is to build your own AI-powered toolkit that gets out of your way—and gets results.

How to Build Your First Daily AI Workflow

If AI is your assistant, then your workflow is your operating manual. It's not enough to know what the tools are—you need to know how to actually use them, day to day, in a way that saves you time and boosts your output. This is where most people stall. They try a tool once, get a mildly interesting result, and never touch it again. Not because it wasn't useful—but because they didn't build it into their routine.

So let's fix that. The first step is simple: pick one part of your day that's predictable and time-consuming. Writing emails, summarizing meetings, planning your week, researching a topic—anything you do often. That's your starting point.

Let's say you're buried in email. You could start every morning with ChatGPT or Claude open next to your inbox. Copy-paste emails you need to respond to and have AI generate polite, professional replies. You tweak them, personalize a sentence or two, and hit send. Ten minutes later, your inbox is cleared, your tone is on point, and you haven't wasted a drop of mental energy crafting the perfect closing line.

Or maybe you have a weekly report to write. Instead of building it from scratch, start with an AI draft. Feed it last week's version, plus new data, and ask for a first pass. Then edit. You'll still bring your brain to the process—but now you're starting from 60% done instead of 0%. Multiply that time saved across weeks, and you've just clawed back hours.

Daily AI workflows don't need to be fancy. A student might use AI to summarize reading assignments and quiz them on key points. A marketer might use it to generate ten headline ideas before lunch. A freelancer might create a prompt template for writing proposals and crank them out in half the time.

The key is consistency. Don't just try it once. Use it every day for a week. Refine how you ask for things. Build prompt templates. Get faster. Notice what works. AI rewards repetition. The more you use it, the better your results—and your instincts—get.

Eventually, your workflow becomes automatic. It's just how you do things. AI becomes part of the system. And that's the real unlock. Not "Wow, this tool is cool," but "This tool makes me better every day."

And yes, you'll hit some bumps. Weird responses. Flawed logic. Bad outputs. That's part of it. Learn to spot the glitches, adjust your input, and move on. You're not aiming for perfect. You're aiming for leveraged.

Start with one task. Build a simple loop: input → AI draft → human tweak → done. That's your first workflow. Then build another. And another.

By the end of the month, you'll be running a system. And that system won't just save time—it'll free up your best energy for the work only you can do.

Case Study: How One Freelancer Doubled Their Income

Meet Sam. Graphic designer. Decent portfolio. Decent clients. Decent money. The problem? Sam was burning out trying to do it all—mockups, client calls, revisions, emails, marketing, invoices, proposals. By the time work was done, there was no energy left to actually grow the business. Sound familiar?

Sam didn't start out trying to "use AI." They just wanted to buy back time. The first step was using ChatGPT to write proposal drafts. Sam would input a few bullet points, let the AI generate the body, then tweak it to match their voice. What used to take 30 minutes per client now took 5. That alone freed up hours every week.

Next came client communications. Sam built a small library of prompt templates for updates, check-ins, and feedback responses. AI helped polish the language, speed up delivery, and reduce the emotional drain of constantly writing "friendly but firm" emails. That mental overhead? Gone.

Then Sam got bold. They started using AI to assist with brainstorming design ideas. Not to generate final work, but to break creative blocks. They'd describe the concept, get AI to suggest directions, color palettes, or layout inspiration, and use that as a jumping-off point. The work stayed original—but the process got way faster.

AI also took over research. Instead of manually digging through endless articles for trends, client industry data, or competitor benchmarks, Sam used Claude to summarize relevant info. Ten pages of reading turned into one paragraph of insights. That alone saved hours of slog and gave Sam a leg up in client strategy.

Within three months, Sam noticed something wild. Revenue had doubled. Not because they raised prices. Not because they worked longer hours. But because they were suddenly doing more client work, faster, with better quality and more energy. Turnaround times dropped. Client satisfaction jumped. Referrals increased. And for the first time in a long time, Sam actually had breathing room.

AI didn't replace Sam. It didn't design the work or close the deals. It just cleared the clutter. It handled the admin, the setup, the blank-page moments that steal momentum. Sam still brought the vision. But now that vision had leverage.

This is what most AI success stories look like—not a robot doing everything, but a person doing more of what they're best at because the rest got streamlined. It's not about being a tech wizard. It's about being strategic.

Whatever your craft, your gig, your grind—there's probably a Sam version of it. And there's probably low-hanging fruit AI can help you pick. Emails. Drafts. Summaries. Planning. Proposals. Research. Content. All the stuff that eats your time while you try to "get to the real work."

If you want more money, more flow, and fewer meltdowns, don't try to hustle harder. Try to work smarter. Like Sam did.

AI isn't just for coders and CEOs. It's for anyone who wants to stop drowning in busywork and start scaling their output. And that can start today.

Why the Smartest Users Treat AI Like a Partner

Here's the mindset shift that separates the casual dabblers from the people actually getting results: they don't treat AI like a toy. They treat it like a teammate. Not a genius. Not a replacement. But a fast, capable assistant that helps them think, create, decide, and execute.

The people getting the most out of AI aren't necessarily the ones who write the cleverest prompts. They're the ones who know how to collaborate. They treat AI like a conversation. A loop. A back-and-forth. They don't expect it to nail the answer on the first try. They expect to refine. They stay curious.

That's the first key: ask better questions. Instead of just saying "write an email," they'll say, "write an email in a warm but confident tone that explains a delay without sounding like an excuse." The more context they give, the better the output. They treat AI like a junior teammate who needs direction, not like a vending machine that spits out genius.

The second key is iteration. They don't stop at the first draft. They ask for three variations. They ask for a rewrite with a different angle. They ask it to punch it up, strip it down, or make it sharper. They know that the gold is often in version three or four, not version one.

They also build habits. They have go-to prompt templates. Saved workflows. Daily routines where AI fits in smoothly—whether it's summarizing meetings, drafting replies, or helping plan next week's agenda. The tech becomes invisible. The results speak for themselves.

And most importantly, they take ownership of the final output. They don't blindly copy-paste. They review. They shape. They infuse their tone, their judgment, their context. AI helps them go faster, but they still steer the ship.

This mindset isn't just more effective—it's more sustainable. Because AI is going to keep evolving. What's clunky today will be seamless tomorrow. What feels like an edge today will be the standard next year. The people who learn to partner with AI now won't just keep up—they'll lead.

Think about it this way: the smartest people in every field don't hoard knowledge. They build systems. They don't do everything themselves—they delegate, automate, and optimize. AI is just the next level of that.

So stop treating it like a gimmick. Start treating it like a collaborator. Let it challenge your thinking. Let it speed up your execution. Let it push your creative boundaries. But don't give it the keys. You're still the one driving.

AI isn't about replacing you. It's about expanding you. Your ideas, your output, your reach. The sooner you start thinking of it as a teammate, the faster you unlock what it can really do.

The smartest users already know this. Now you do too.

Why Prompting Isn't a Magic Spell (Sorry, TikTok)

You've seen the videos. Someone types a single line into ChatGPT, hits enter, and out comes a flawless business plan, bestselling novel, or six-figure side hustle. It looks like magic. But here's the truth: most of those results are cherry-picked, heavily edited, or straight-up fiction.

Prompting isn't a superpower. It's a skill. And like any skill, it gets better with practice, context, and a little patience. If you treat AI like a mind reader, it'll disappoint you. If you treat it like a smart intern who needs clear direction, it'll blow your mind.

The myth of the perfect prompt has gotten out of hand. People spend more time searching for secret phrases than actually using the tool. They think there's some hidden combination of words that will unlock next-level results, like a cheat code in a video game. The reality is much less glamorous—and much more useful.

A good prompt is just a clear instruction. Nothing mystical. You're giving the AI a job. Your job is to be the manager: explain what you want, define the outcome, and give it enough information to work with. That's it. No magic words. Just clarity.

Let's say you want help writing a blog post. You could say, "Write a blog post about productivity." That'll give you something, sure—but probably something bland and generic. Try instead: "Write a 500-word blog post in a conversational tone that compares traditional productivity tips with unexpected strategies used by high-performing creatives. Include a funny anecdote and end with a clear takeaway."

See the difference? You're not hoping for a miracle. You're giving direction. And if it's not quite right on the first try? Cool. Ask it to tweak the tone. Expand a section. Focus more on a specific example. It's not about getting it perfect instantly. It's about collaborating until it's right.

The other trap is overloading your prompt with jargon or trying to sound smart. AI doesn't need fancy words. It needs clear ones. You're not impressing it. You're instructing it. Keep it simple. Talk to it like you're explaining a task to someone who wants to help but doesn't know your context—yet.

And here's a fun bonus: the more you prompt, the more you learn about your own thinking. What do you actually want? What matters most in this task? What tone are you going for? Prompting well forces clarity. That clarity? It's useful even outside the AI.

So forget the prompt porn. You don't need a magic spell. You need a mindset. Be specific. Be iterative. Treat the AI like a partner, not a psychic. The results will speak for themselves.

AI isn't reading your mind. It's reading your instructions. The better you give them, the better the tool performs. That's not magic. That's skill. And anyone can learn it. Starting now.

The 80/20 of Prompting That Actually Works

You don't need to master every prompt trick in the book. You just need to master the few that matter. Like most things, prompting follows the 80/20 rule: 80% of your results will come from 20% of your effort—if you focus on the right moves.

First, the golden rule: always give context. The more background you give the AI, the better it can generate relevant responses. Think tone, audience, format, and purpose. Instead of saying, "Write a summary," say, "Summarize this article in two paragraphs for busy marketing professionals who want the big ideas without fluff." Same task. Better output.

Second, be specific about format. If you want a list, ask for a list. If you want three options, say so. If you want something written like a tweet, make that clear. You're not being demanding—you're giving structure. AI thrives on structure. You're not just asking for content; you're shaping the frame it's built inside.

Third, use examples. This is where prompting gets powerful. If you want the AI to mimic your voice, give it a sample. If you want a certain kind of analysis, show it what you mean. One strong example can teach the model more than a thousand vague words. Copy, paste, and say, "Write something like this."

Fourth, work in iterations. Start simple, then refine. Don't expect a masterpiece on the first go. Get something basic, then say, "Now make it punchier," or "Add a case study," or "Cut the fluff and make it sharper." You're co-writing, not vending.

Fifth—and this is a big one—reuse your prompts. Build a prompt library. Save the ones that work. Create templates for tasks you do often: weekly updates, email outreach, ad copy, blog intros, meeting agendas. Don't start from scratch every time. This turns prompting into a system, not just a stunt.

You can even turn basic prompts into workflows. Let's say you're writing a newsletter. Step one: "Give me three newsletter topic ideas for solopreneurs." Step two: "Outline the best one." Step three: "Write a 200-word intro in a relatable tone." Step four: "Suggest a call-to-action that fits this tone and topic." Boom—done.

This is where the 80/20 kicks in. You're not trying to be clever. You're trying to be clear. You're not prompting for perfection. You're prompting for progress. The best users don't treat AI like a black box. They treat it like a toolkit.

So forget the gimmicks. Forget the tweet threads that promise "secret prompts billionaires use." The only prompt you need is the one that gets the job done—and that usually means clarity, structure, and iteration.

Master those, and you won't just get better results. You'll think better. Write faster. Work smarter. And that's the real magic.

Not prompt hacks. Prompt habits.

Plug-and-Play Prompt Templates That Save Time

You don't need to reinvent the wheel every time you talk to an AI. In fact, if you are, you're doing it wrong. The smartest users don't just write good prompts—they build great templates. Plug-and-play formats that can be reused, refined, and repurposed to save brainpower and get consistent results.

Think of prompt templates like macros for your creativity. Instead of staring at a blank screen, you start with a framework. It's not cheating—it's working smarter. And once you have a few reliable ones, your workflow starts humming.

Let's say you're writing content. One go-to template could be: "Write a [length] [type of content] on [topic] for [audience] in a [tone] tone. Include [specific request or structure]." You fill in the blanks, hit go, and tweak from there. Want a LinkedIn post? A cold email? A podcast intro? This formula flexes with you.

Need to summarize a wall of text? Try: "Summarize the following [type of document] for a [specific audience]. Highlight key insights and cut unnecessary fluff. Keep it under [X] words."

Doing research? Use: "Based on the following prompt, provide a concise overview of the topic, current trends, and 2-3 key insights: [insert question]. Respond in bullet points."

Want to refine your writing? "Rewrite this text to make it more [tone: clear, punchy, persuasive, etc.]. Keep the meaning the same but improve readability."

Creating marketing copy? Here's a reliable one: "Write three variations of a [type of ad copy] for [product/service]. Focus on [benefit or hook]. Make it [tone]. Include a strong CTA."

The beauty of templates is that they're endlessly customizable. Once you have a few, you stop wasting time typing the same instructions over and over. You just plug in your variables—topic, tone, audience—and let the system run.

You can keep your templates in a doc, a notes app, or a dedicated AI workspace. Name them clearly. Tag them by use case. Eventually, you'll have a personal library of prompts for everything from brainstorming to branding to babysitting your calendar.

And don't be afraid to remix what works. If you find a prompt that gives you gold, copy it and tweak the structure. Turn it into a new template. If something flops, revise it. Prompting is iterative, and templates evolve with you.

Best of all, this approach turns AI from a guessing game into a process. No more "let's see what it gives me." You're setting the rules. You're choosing the format. You're leading the conversation.

Plug-and-play doesn't mean lazy. It means leveraged. It means having a toolkit you can count on when your brain is fried, your deadlines are tight, or your creative engine needs a jumpstart.

Stop starting from zero. Start from a template. That's how pros use AI.

Simple. Scalable. Repeatable. And way more fun.

Getting AI to Match Your Voice + Style

The moment AI starts writing for you, the question becomes: how do you make sure it still sounds like you? Because the last thing anyone wants is to read something that screams, "Hello, I am a robot pretending to be human."

The trick isn't to dumb things down. It's to train your AI tools to reflect your voice. And yes, it's totally possible. You just need to give it the right ingredients.

Start with samples. Pull together a few pieces of your own writing that sound unmistakably like you—emails, posts, reports, intros, rants. Doesn't matter what the format is, as long as it's authentically yours. Feed that into your AI and say, "Analyze this and mimic the tone, sentence structure, and word choice."

Then, when you're prompting, add that reference. Say something like, "Write this in my voice, similar to the style of the previous example. Keep it casual, sharp, and mildly sarcastic." Be honest about your tone. If you swear a little, say so. If you like short, punchy sentences, note that. The AI doesn't judge. It just adapts.

The next level is building a voice profile. Describe yourself in your prompt: "I write in a friendly, no-fluff tone that's humorous but grounded. I prefer contractions, avoid buzzwords, and speak like I'm talking to a smart friend at 2 a.m." Now tell the AI to follow those rules in everything it creates for you.

Consistency is key. The more you write with AI and correct its output, the more you shape its responses. If a phrase feels off, tweak it. Then tell the AI what you changed and why. It learns from the feedback loop. You're not just editing—you're training.

Don't be afraid to go meta. Say, "This sounds too generic. Make it more specific and use my typical metaphors." Or, "This feels too formal. Rewrite it like I'm giving advice over coffee." The AI's strength is iteration. Use it.

Another move? Build tone templates. If you often write in different styles—let's say one for clients, one for social, and one for internal docs—create a short description for each. Then use those as add-ons in your prompts. Example: "Use my client-friendly tone: warm, professional, helpful, no jargon." Keep those labels handy. It saves time and keeps your voice tight.

And yes, you'll still need to polish. AI can get close—sometimes scarily close—but it's not perfect. Final tweaks matter. You're the filter. You're the taste. Don't let AI flatten your style just to make it efficient.

The goal isn't to sound like a machine. It's to sound like you, but faster, sharper, and more scalable. When your audience reads something and thinks, "Yep, that's totally their voice," you'll know you nailed it.

Use AI to amplify your voice—not replace it. That's the real flex.

Teaching AI Your Systems (Without Losing Your Mind)

It's one thing to get AI to write in your voice. It's another to get it to think like you—or at least follow your process. Whether you're running a business, managing a team, writing content, or organizing your life, chances are you have systems. The way you handle tasks. The steps you always follow. The checklist in your head.

Teaching those systems to AI can feel overwhelming. But it doesn't have to be. You don't need to hand over a company playbook. You just need to start simple: define the rules, break things into steps, and train the tool one piece at a time.

Let's say you run a content calendar. You have a method—topic research on Mondays, draft by Wednesday, publish Friday. You use specific formats, word counts, and tones for different platforms. Instead of explaining this every time, document it once in a prompt. "Here's how I plan and execute content weekly. Follow this process every time I ask you to create a post." Then feed it a few examples.

Want it to help with hiring? Write out your screening process: what you look for, the questions you ask, the red flags to watch. Then create a prompt like, "Act as my hiring assistant. Use this process to evaluate the following resume or candidate." The AI won't replace your judgment, but it can pre-filter and surface patterns you might miss.

If you're a solopreneur or freelancer juggling client work, teach AI your client onboarding system. How you ask for info. What templates you send. What steps you follow. It could be as simple as, "When I say 'kickoff email,' generate this email template with a personalized greeting and a three-step onboarding checklist." You're not reinventing your process. You're just plugging it into a helper that remembers it every time.

You can also use AI to enforce discipline on your messiest systems. Let's be real—some of us have systems in our head that fall apart on paper. Use AI to clean them up. Say, "Help me turn this chaotic to-do list into a weekly execution plan with priorities and due dates." Or, "Help me write SOPs based on the way I usually do things."

The point isn't perfection. It's repeatability. Every time you teach AI part of your process, you save future-you a headache. You create leverage. You move from improvising to executing.

You don't need to train it on everything at once. Just start with one thing. Document it. Prompt it. Test it. Refine. Bit by bit, the AI learns your systems. And the more it learns, the less you waste time explaining, retyping, or fixing.

You're not just using AI to think faster—you're teaching it how you think. And that's where the power kicks in. Because when your systems live outside your brain, they stop being bottlenecks. They start being assets.

Teach your systems once. Use them forever. That's how you scale yourself without cloning yourself.

Will Robots Take My Job? (Short Answer: Kinda)

Every time a new technology hits the scene, the question comes up: is this going to take my job? AI is no different. And let's not sugarcoat it—yeah, some jobs are going to change a lot. Some will shrink. Some will disappear. But the full story isn't doom and gloom. It's more like a remix: parts of your job will get automated, but that also means new roles, new tools, and a whole new way to show your value.

If your job involves anything repetitive, predictable, or easily explained with a checklist, then AI probably has its eye on it. Data entry. Basic customer service. Low-level analysis. These are already being automated—not because AI is evil, but because it's cheaper, faster, and available 24/7. Businesses aren't looking to replace people for the fun of it. They're looking to cut friction. And AI is frictionless.

But here's the twist: the more your job involves judgment, creativity, nuance, or empathy, the harder it is to replace you. AI can summarize a contract, but it can't negotiate a deal. It can suggest a headline, but it can't capture the human nuance behind a brand. It can answer questions, but it can't lead a team, handle messy human dynamics, or build trust.

What's more likely is that your job will evolve. You'll delegate the dull parts to AI and spend more time on high-impact work. If you're a writer, you'll use AI to generate rough drafts so you can focus on editing and strategy. If you're a teacher, you'll automate lesson prep and spend more time connecting with students. If you're a manager, you'll use AI to handle scheduling, reporting, and coordination so you can lead instead of babysit logistics.

But this only works if you adapt. The people who panic or resist will struggle. The people who learn to work with AI will thrive. Not because they're better at tech—but because they're better at thinking, learning, and collaborating. You don't have to become a coder. You just have to get curious, try things, and figure out what makes you irreplaceable.

Here's a way to think about it: AI doesn't take jobs. It takes tasks. If you understand the difference, you can protect yourself. Break your job into parts. Ask: what's automatable? What's uniquely human? Then double down on the human part. That's where your leverage lives.

The job market's not collapsing. It's shifting. Some roles will vanish. Others will explode. New industries will be built around AI tools, training, ethics, integration, and innovation. The question isn't, "Will I lose my job?" It's, "Am I learning faster than the world is changing?"

The short answer: yeah, robots might take part of your job. But if you're smart, you'll use that as an opportunity—not an obituary.

Because the future belongs to the people who know how to work with machines—not fear them.

Framework: Automate, Augment, Adapt

If you're wondering how to stay valuable in an AI-powered world, here's the answer in three words: Automate, Augment, Adapt. It's not a buzzword sandwich. It's a framework. And it works whether you're a freelancer, a founder, or someone just trying not to fall behind.

Let's start with Automate. Look at your work like a detective at a crime scene: what's repeatable? What's boring? What makes you say, "This again?" That's the stuff AI should take over. Data cleanup. Calendar juggling. Inbox sorting. Initial drafts. Research summaries. Scheduling. All the low-brain, high-friction tasks that drain your day but don't require your judgment. If you can write a step-by-step for it, you can probably automate part of it.

Next is Augment. This is where things get interesting. Augmentation means using AI to level up your work, not just replace grunt tasks. It's like putting your brain on steroids—but ethical. Think: using AI to help you brainstorm, pressure test decisions, generate design options, polish proposals, and turn raw ideas into refined assets. It's you doing the thinking, but with backup. Like having a research assistant, a writing coach, and a strategist on speed dial.

The final move is Adapt. This is where you stop playing defense and start playing offense. Adaptation means actively reshaping how you work—how you learn, how you deliver value, how you position your skills. It's keeping pace with how your industry is changing. You watch what's working. You test new tools. You ask better questions. You look for new problems to solve and new ways to solve them. You evolve.

People get stuck because they think adaptation means becoming someone else. It doesn't. It just means upgrading the version of you that's already there. The curious version. The creative version. The one who's not afraid to let go of old habits if something better comes along.

This framework—Automate, Augment, Adapt—isn't just about survival. It's about strategy. It keeps you focused on leverage. It protects your time. And it turns AI from a threat into a cheat code.

You don't need to master this all at once. Just pick one. Automate one thing this week. Augment one piece of your work. Try one new way of doing something you've always done the same way. Tiny shifts lead to big advantages when everyone else is standing still.

The people who will thrive in the next decade won't be the ones who know the most—they'll be the ones who move the fastest. Not blindly. Not recklessly. But with a mindset built for change. This framework gives you that.

Automate what slows you down. Augment what makes you better. Adapt so you stay useful.

That's how you stay ahead. Not by doing more. But by doing smarter.

Skills That Actually Future-Proof You

Everyone's talking about future-proofing. But let's get real: most of what's sold as "future-proof" is vague advice wrapped in tech jargon. Learn to code. Pivot to STEM. Become a data ninja. Sure, those things help—but they're not the full picture. What actually future-proofs you in the age of AI isn't just technical skill. It's a mix of mindset, adaptability, and a few killer meta-skills that play well with machines and humans.

Start with critical thinking. Not sexy, but essential. In a world drowning in AI-generated content, you need to be the one who can sift through the noise, spot the BS, and ask better questions. AI is great at giving you answers. But it sucks at knowing which questions matter. That's your job. The people who can frame problems clearly—and challenge lazy assumptions—are the ones who stay in demand.

Next is communication. Not just writing well. Communicating clearly, across mediums, for different audiences. If you can take a complex idea, strip it of fluff, and deliver it in a way that makes people care—you win. Whether you're selling a product, pitching a project, or leading a team, that's a power move. And it gets more valuable as AI floods the zone with generic, wordy garbage.

Then there's creativity. And no, not just painting or playing guitar. Creativity in the sense of lateral thinking. Connecting dots others don't see. Coming up with fresh angles, new solutions, better ways. AI is great at remixing what already exists. But it struggles with true originality. Your edge is the weird thought no one else had. Nurture that.

Also, emotional intelligence. Soft skills are becoming hard currency. The ability to read a room, defuse conflict, manage egos, and lead without micromanaging? AI can't touch that. Teams still need humans who know how to talk to other humans. Especially when things get tense, weird, or ambiguous—which, in the future of work, is always.

And finally: learning agility. The ability to pick up new tools, adapt to new environments, and stay curious under pressure. This isn't about memorizing facts—it's about being coachable, flexible, and experimental. The best AI users aren't the ones who "know everything." They're the ones who figure things out quickly, test without fear, and evolve in real time.

Put it together and you get a stack of skills that scale. These aren't tied to one job, one industry, or one tool. They're portable. Durable. And they make you harder to replace.

So yeah, learn how to use AI. Learn your tools. But also double down on what makes you irreplaceable: judgment, clarity, originality, empathy, and the ability to keep learning faster than the world changes.

That's the real upgrade. Not just future-proofing your job. Future-proofing you.

How to Make Money with AI (Without Selling Your Soul)

Let's talk money. Not hype, not crypto-style fantasies, but real ways people are using AI to earn—without turning into scammy influencers or soulless automation zombies. Because yes, there's cash on the table. But the goal isn't to sell your soul to the algorithm. It's to use AI as a lever that amplifies what you already do well.

Start with what you know. AI isn't some magic business in a box. You don't need to become an "AI entrepreneur" overnight. You need to look at what you're already good at—design, writing, coaching, teaching, organizing, selling—and ask: how can AI help me do this faster, better, or at scale?

Writers are using AI to draft first versions, brainstorm titles, generate outlines, or even repurpose content across formats. A single blog post becomes a newsletter, a tweet thread, a LinkedIn post, and a podcast script—with the help of a few prompt tweaks and a trained assistant on the backend. It's not lazy. It's leveraged.

Designers are using image generation tools like Midjourney or DALL•E to mock up ideas, create fast concepts for clients, or build assets for social media. It's not replacing their taste or skill—it's speeding up the boring part so they can focus on the polish.

Course creators and educators are using AI to script lessons, generate quiz questions, build slide decks, and write marketing emails. Coaches use it to prep sessions, brainstorm frameworks, or personalize outreach at scale. If your work involves content, communication, or problem-solving, AI can multiply your effort without multiplying your hours.

Even small business owners are getting in on it. Automating customer responses. Speeding up lead gen. Running smarter ads. Writing better product descriptions. Building chatbots that actually make sense. You don't need a tech team—you need curiosity and a few hours on YouTube.

What you want to avoid is chasing the trend with no plan. "Starting an AI agency" sounds cool until you realize you don't know how to sell, service, or deliver consistently. The money's in the execution, not the branding. Use AI to solve real problems for real people, and you'll never run out of ways to earn.

If you're just starting out, don't overthink it. Pick a problem you can solve. Use AI to speed up your solution. Charge fairly. Deliver well. Repeat. Over time, you build a stack of offers, systems, and workflows that do more with less.

Making money with AI isn't about becoming a prompt guru. It's about building a flywheel. Create value, use AI to scale or streamline that value, then reinvest the time and energy you save into higher-leverage work.

Don't sell your soul. Sell smart solutions. Let AI do the heavy lifting so you can focus on what actually matters: results, relationships, and repeat business.

That's how you get paid. And stay human doing it.

How Small Biz Owners Are Scaling with AI

If you're running a small business, chances are you're juggling twelve jobs at once. You're the marketer, the customer service rep, the bookkeeper, the project manager, and somehow still expected to deliver on the actual product or service. AI won't eliminate all of that overnight—but it can chop the chaos in half.

The smartest small biz owners aren't waiting for the perfect AI tool to fall from the sky. They're already using what's available to do more with less, serve more customers without burning out, and scale without hiring a small army.

Start with customer service. Tools like chatbots or email assistants powered by AI can handle common questions, route issues to the right place, and even handle basic troubleshooting. No more drowning in inbox replies or answering the same three questions every day. You get time back, and your customers get faster responses.

Then there's marketing. AI can generate Instagram captions, write email newsletters, draft ad copy, and help you brainstorm fresh campaign angles in minutes. No need to stare at a blank screen wondering what to post. Some business owners even use AI to analyze past content performance and suggest what's likely to hit again.

Sales? Same deal. You can use AI to score leads, personalize follow-ups, and build proposal templates that update automatically based on client info. One wedding planner used ChatGPT to rewrite their pricing guide in a friendlier tone—and started getting more inquiries without changing a single number.

Even operations get a glow-up. Inventory management, invoicing, appointment scheduling—all of it can be semi-automated with the right combo of AI tools and basic integrations. The goal isn't full automation. It's to stop wasting precious brainpower on stuff that doesn't move the needle.

One boutique owner started using AI to help plan her buying schedule. She'd input past sales, seasonality, and current trends, then have the AI generate suggestions for what to stock next. Her hit rate on inventory doubled. Another used AI to write product descriptions that matched her brand voice, freeing up hours every launch.

The common thread? These aren't tech wizards. They're resourceful, curious people who got tired of doing everything manually. They looked at their business and asked, "Where am I repeating myself? Where am I guessing when I could be deciding with data? Where could a robot help me show up better?"

You don't need to be cutting-edge. You need to be practical. Plug AI into the cracks where time leaks out. Use it to show up faster, more consistently, and with more focus on the parts of your business only you can do.

Scaling isn't always about growing bigger. Sometimes it's about growing smarter. That's what AI offers: leverage. Not a miracle. A multiplier.

Start small. Start now. Let the tools help you breathe again.

And when your biz starts running like it's got an extra pair of hands? You'll know it's working..

What's Coming Next (Without the Sci-Fi Nonsense)

If you Google the future of AI, you'll find two extremes: utopian fantasy or apocalyptic doom. Flying cars and robot therapists. Jobless wastelands and sentient machines plotting revenge. Entertaining? Sure. Useful? Not even close.

The real future of AI is way messier—and way more human. It won't look like a sci-fi movie. It'll look like your daily tools quietly getting smarter. Your apps anticipating your needs. Your devices doing more without you even noticing. It's less "Skynet" and more "Hey, that calendar invite just scheduled itself."

Let's start with the obvious: AI isn't slowing down. It's speeding up. Tools are improving fast. What felt groundbreaking six months ago already feels clunky. The models are getting faster, more accurate, and more context-aware. Expect tools that remember your preferences, understand your voice, and get better the more you use them—without having to start from scratch every time.

You'll also see AI becoming invisible. Right now, we know when we're using ChatGPT or Midjourney. But soon, AI will just be baked into everything. Your word processor will suggest whole paragraphs. Your email app will rewrite replies before you've typed a word. Your meeting software will create action plans while you're still talking. The tools disappear, and all that's left is the output.

Jobs will shift. Not disappear overnight—but shift. Roles that are purely mechanical or repetitive will keep shrinking. But new roles will emerge around managing AI, training models, ensuring outputs are ethical, or designing human-AI collaboration systems. Entire industries will be built around making AI safer, faster, and easier to integrate. Think of it like the rise of the internet—painful at first, chaotic in the middle, and impossible to live without by the end.

Regulation is coming too. Slowly, awkwardly, but inevitably. Countries and companies are realizing that AI isn't just another app—it affects privacy, bias, labor, and power structures. Expect more oversight, more compliance requirements, and more conversations about what's fair, what's risky, and who's responsible when AI screws up.

And yes, there will be moments that feel weird. Tools making decisions you didn't expect. Content that sounds real but isn't. Misinformation at scale. It'll be messy. But messiness is where progress lives. Our job isn't to be unbothered. Our job is to stay awake, stay smart, and keep asking, "What do I want this technology to do for me?"

Because that's the future: not one we watch unfold, but one we shape by how we use the tools. AI isn't destiny. It's design.

So don't wait for the singularity. Don't obsess over the next big model drop. Stay grounded. Stay useful. The real future isn't flashy—it's functional.

And it's already here, creeping into your calendar, rewriting your to-do list, and helping you get through Monday without losing your mind. More magic, less noise. That's what's coming next.

Keeping Up Without Doomscrolling

Staying updated on AI feels like drinking from a firehose while scrolling through a panic attack. One minute it's breakthrough news, the next it's layoffs, lawsuits, and a new model that "changes everything." It's easy to feel overwhelmed, underprepared, and one headline away from total existential dread. But here's the truth: you don't need to follow everything to stay ahead—you just need to follow the right things, in the right way.

First rule: kill the doomscroll. Mindless consumption of tech news will not make you smarter—it'll just make you anxious. You don't need to know about every new paper, startup, or model drop the minute it happens. Most of it won't matter in a week. Some of it won't matter at all. Filter before you absorb.

Start by curating your sources. Pick 2–3 trusted voices who break things down in plain English. Not hype merchants. Not doomsayers. Just smart, clear thinkers who understand the tech and the context. Think newsletters, YouTube explainers, or podcasts that respect your time and don't talk down to you. Follow them consistently. Skip the rest.

Then schedule your learning. Instead of randomly clicking through your feed, carve out a weekly "AI catch-up" block. Read summaries. Watch a video. Try one new tool. Stay curious—but stay in control. The goal is not to binge on information. It's to integrate what actually matters into your work and life.

Use your tools to help you filter. Have ChatGPT summarize that 40-page white paper. Use Claude to pull key points from the latest OpenAI blog post. Let AI handle the overload so you don't have to. It's not cheating—it's how smart people stay sane.

And learn in public. Share what you're experimenting with. Post your takeaways. Teach someone else. You don't need to be an expert to be helpful. You just need to be one step ahead. Teaching reinforces learning. Plus, it builds a reputation. And in an AI-powered world, your ability to think clearly and share that clarity is worth more than ever.

Most importantly, give yourself permission to not know everything. You're not a machine. You're not supposed to keep up with every update in real time. Even the people building this stuff are constantly playing catch-up. Your job is to stay relevant, not perfect.

So stop chasing every headline. Start building a rhythm that works for you. AI isn't a sprint—it's a long game. And staying in the game means managing your energy, not just your knowledge.

Be curious. Be selective. Be kind to your brain.

Because keeping up shouldn't mean burning out.

It should mean moving forward—calm, clear, and ready for whatever's next.

Build a Personal AI Stack That Grows With You

You don't need to use every AI tool on the internet. You just need a small, solid stack—the digital equivalent of a pocketknife—that works for how you think, work, and create. Something that supports your workflow, not overwhelms it. And the key? Start small, then evolve.

A personal AI stack is just a collection of tools you actually use. Not the ones you signed up for and forgot. Not the ones influencers hype for clicks. The ones that quietly save you time, boost your output, or help you think better. Think of them like your digital pit crew—always there, tuned to your needs, and ready to help you move faster without burning out.

Begin with three categories: thinking, creating, and organizing. For thinking, you want a tool that helps you brainstorm, explore ideas, and break down complex topics. Something like ChatGPT, Claude, or Perplexity—whatever helps you ask better questions and get better answers.

For creating, choose tools that help you generate, refine, or repurpose. This might be writing assistants, image generators, audio editors, or even code copilots. You don't need all of them. Just the one or two that help you make stuff faster, better, and with less friction.

And for organizing, look for tools that help you track ideas, manage projects, or systematize your life. Think Notion, Tana, or even AI-enhanced calendars and to-do apps. These are the glue that holds your stack together—the ones that keep things from falling through the cracks.

Once you've got your core stack, test it. Don't commit to tools you haven't stress-tested. Set a 30-day rule: if it doesn't prove its value in your workflow within a month, it's out. You're building a system, not a graveyard of logins.

Then, as your needs evolve, your stack evolves. Got more clients? Add a content repurposing tool. Starting a podcast? Try AI editing or show note generation. Launching a product? Use AI to draft landing pages, create visuals, and build out marketing funnels. Your stack grows with your ambition—but only if you let it.

Don't worry about having the flashiest setup. Worry about having the right one. The stack that fits your habits, your goals, your brain. The tools that quietly get things done so you can focus on what actually matters.

And remember: integration beats complication. It's better to go deep with a few tools than to get scattered across twenty. Simplicity is power. Pick tools that talk to each other. Tools you can trust. Tools you'll still want to use six months from now.

Your AI stack doesn't need to be impressive. It needs to be yours.

Build it. Refine it. Let it grow with you.

That's how you stop chasing shiny objects—and start building real momentum.

Create Your Own AI Philosophy

If you're going to live in a world surrounded by AI, you might as well have a point of view about it. Not just "I use ChatGPT sometimes," but a real philosophy—a personal filter for what you'll use, what you'll avoid, and how you want this technology to work for you, not on you.

Your AI philosophy doesn't need to be complicated. It just needs to be honest. Start with this: what do you want AI to do for you? Save time? Spark ideas? Make you more productive, more creative, more focused? Good. Write that down. Make it real. Then check every tool and workflow against it. If it doesn't move you in that direction, it doesn't belong in your stack.

Next, define your boundaries. What are you not okay with? Blindly trusting output without review? Using AI to cut corners in ways that compromise your integrity? Automating personal connections? Everyone has a line. Know yours. Otherwise, tech will draw it for you—and it usually draws it around profit, not people.

A solid AI philosophy also includes how you'll handle friction. Things will break. Outputs will suck. Data will disappear. Are you the type who ditches tools at the first glitch? Or do you commit to learning, iterating, improving the prompts, improving yourself? Knowing your attitude toward failure will shape how much you actually benefit from these tools.

Your philosophy should evolve, too. The AI space moves fast. What made sense last year might feel off today. That's fine. Growth is part of the deal. Revisit your philosophy once in a while and ask: is this still serving me? Am I in control, or just keeping up for the sake of it? Use that gut check to reset.

Also: you don't need to explain your philosophy to anyone. But you should be able to. It keeps you intentional. Are you using AI to unlock more time with your kids? To reduce burnout? To prototype new ideas faster? To sharpen your creative edge? Own that. When you know your why, the how gets a lot easier.

The goal here isn't to get philosophical for the sake of it. It's to stay grounded. With every new wave of tech, there's a risk of losing the plot—chasing every trend, automating for automation's sake, outsourcing your actual thinking. Your philosophy is what keeps you human in the loop.

So make one. Make it yours. Doesn't have to be perfect. Doesn't have to be public. It just has to be true.

Use AI to build a better version of your life—not someone else's.

That's your north star. The rest is just software.

Your Sanity-First AI Action Plan

You've made it through the firehose. Myths busted. Tools tested. Prompts sharpened. Now what? It's time to make this real. Not in a hustle-bro way. Not in a "grind harder, scale faster" way. In a sanity-first, practical, human way. An action plan that doesn't burn you out but builds you up.

Start by picking one thing. Just one. One tool, one workflow, one prompt that makes your life easier or your work smoother. Don't try to become an AI power user overnight. That's how you get overwhelmed and quit. Find the small win. Maybe it's using ChatGPT to write outlines faster. Maybe it's setting up an AI email assistant. Maybe it's just getting your notes organized with an AI-powered workspace. One move, one win.

Then block time to play. Literally. Block it on your calendar. "AI Play Time—30 minutes." No pressure. No deadlines. Just exploring, testing, asking questions, and seeing what happens. This is how you build intuition. This is how you learn what these tools can really do. You don't need to become an expert—you just need to get comfortable.

Next, build a repeatable habit. Something weekly. A Friday review using AI. A Monday brainstorm session. A Wednesday prompt test. Doesn't matter when. Just make it part of your rhythm. You're not adding another chore. You're upgrading something you already do.

Keep a running doc of what works. Save your best prompts. Screenshot your wins. Bookmark the tools that feel right. You're building a personal library here. This isn't just tech—it's your toolkit. Treat it like one.

And finally, check in with yourself every month. Ask: is this helping? Is this saving me time, giving me clarity, making me better at what matters? Or am I just collecting tools for the dopamine hit? If it's not moving the needle, cut it. This plan only works if it works for you.

This isn't about getting ahead of everyone else. It's about staying aligned with yourself while the world changes. It's about building leverage without losing your soul. It's about turning AI into something that supports your goals—not something that replaces your instincts.

You don't need to know everything. You just need to stay in motion. Learn. Apply. Adjust. Repeat. That's the whole game.

And when it feels like too much? Zoom out. Take a breath. Remind yourself: you're not here to become a machine. You're here to use machines to become more you.

Sanity first. Always.

Now go build something great—and let the robots help..

The Future's Not Waiting

You made it. Not just through this—but through the noise. The hype. The fear. The headlines designed to rattle you. What you've got now isn't just knowledge. It's leverage.

AI isn't coming. It's already here. Quietly weaving itself into your calendar, your inbox, your to-do list. The question isn't whether you'll use it. It's whether you'll use it well.

The good news? You don't need to be a tech genius. You don't need to hustle 24/7. You just need to stay curious, stay practical, and treat this stuff like the tool it is. Build workflows that fit your brain. Use prompts that sound like your voice. Choose sanity over speed, clarity over complexity.

The people who win with AI won't be the loudest. They'll be the most intentional. The ones who ask better questions, test smarter systems, and keep their humanity front and center.

This was your launchpad. What you do next? That's the real story.

So close the tab. Open the tool. Try the prompt. Fix the workflow. Send the thing. Tweak. Repeat.

And when the world changes again—and it will—you'll be ready.

Not because you have all the answers.

But because you've learned how to ask the right questions.

Go build.

Stay sharp.

Stay human.

Don't miss out!

Visit the website below and you can sign up to receive emails whenever Leila Brandt publishes a new book. There's no charge and no obligation.

https://books2read.com/r/B-A-PJUUE-UUVQH

BOOKS 2 READ

Connecting independent readers to independent writers.

Did you love *How to Use AI for Work, Money and Productivity: Smart Tools and Prompts to Save Time, Earn More and Stay Sane*? Then you should read *How to Get Organized: Stop Drowning in Chaos, Simplify Everything, and Take Back Your Time and Sanity*[1] by Jonas E. Hales!

[2]

If your life feels like one giant mess — you're not lazy, broken, or doomed. You just need a system that works for your brain.

Get Organized (Even If You're Drowning in Chaos) is the ultimate anti-perfectionist guide to taking control of your space, time, and tasks — even if your laundry's in piles, your to-do list is on fire, and your brain's screaming "nope" every time you try to start.

This book isn't about color-coding your spice rack or alphabetizing your closet. It's about real-world organization for people with messy lives, busy schedules, ADHD brains, executive dysfunction, and zero energy to spare. Whether you're juggling work, parenting, school, neurodivergence, or just

---

1. https://books2read.com/u/bPrY2l

2. https://books2read.com/u/bPrY2l

nonstop overwhelm, this guide helps you go from chaos to clarity without burning out.

Inside, you'll learn how to organize your life when you're completely overwhelmed and don't know where to begin. You'll discover the exact steps to get your physical and digital clutter under control, how to stop task-switching yourself into paralysis, and how to build routines that actually stick — even if you've failed at every planner and productivity hack in the past.

You'll get low-energy systems that still work on bad brain days, a method to beat "start-up dread," and ways to trick your executive function into playing nice. This isn't about becoming perfectly tidy. It's about becoming functional, clear-headed, and in control — finally.

If you've ever whispered "I'm drowning" while looking at your email inbox, kitchen sink, or calendar, this book is your lifeline.

www.ingramcontent.com/pod-product-compliance
Lightning Source LLC
LaVergne TN
LVHW090333210926
848480LV00004B/1400
9798232360801